BIG, FAST RIDES

Alison Hawes

Titles in First Flight

J791.
068

Badger Publishing Limited
15 Wedgwood Gate, Pin Green Industrial Estate,
Stevenage, Hertfordshire SG1 4SU
Telephone: 01438 356907. Fax: 01438 747015
www.badger-publishing.co.uk
enquiries@badger-publishing.co.uk

Big, Fast Rides ISBN 1 84424 824 0

Text © Alison Hawes 2006
Complete work © Badger Publishing Limited 2006

Series Editor: Jonny Zucker
Publisher: David Jamieson
Commissioning Editor: Carrie Lewis
Editor: Paul Martin
Design: Fiona Grant
Cover photography: Kingda Ka © coasterclub.org
Illustration: Laszlo Veres and Ian West
Printed and bound in China through Colorcraft Ltd., Hong Kong

BIG, FAST RIDES
Alison Hawes

Contents

Lots of big parks have rollercoasters.
These are giant rides that look a
bit like trains on very funny tracks.

People like rollercoasters because they are big, fast and fun – and a little bit scary!

Some people like rollercoasters because they like to go fast.

This is the fastest rollercoaster in the world. It was made in the USA in 2005. It can go at 128 miles an hour!

Other people like to be scared by a sudden drop, or by going upside-down.

Kingda Ka rollercoaster,
6 Flags Great Adventure, New Jersey USA

This boy is talking about his favourite rollercoaster.

"It went up really high, and when it stopped it felt as if we were in the air.

"Then we rolled forwards, slowly at first, then WHOOSH down a steep hill. It pulled my face into funny shapes.

"Then we went upside-down. I could feel it but I couldn't see. I had my eyes shut!

"It was very exciting."

As more and more rollercoasters are made, they get bigger and faster – and a lot more scary!

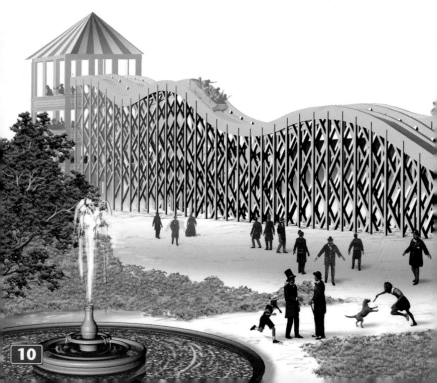

The first rollercoaster was made in the USA. It was made over 120 years ago. It was made of wood.

It went at just 6 miles an hour!

Lots of people liked the first rollercoaster. So more rollercoasters were made.

At first they were all made of wood, like this one.

Giant Dipper, San Diego, USA

Some of the first rollercoasters came off the tracks.

But, in 1912, this man invented a new kind of wheel to keep rollercoasters on the tracks.

Then lots of big, fast, wooden rollercoasters were made.

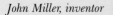

John Miller, inventor

This big wooden rollercoaster was made in 1927. It went at 60 miles an hour.

Cyclone, Crystal Beach, Canada

But it had such big dips and bends that some people passed out on it! It was pulled down in 1946.

More and more wooden rollercoasters were pulled down in the next 25 years.

New rollercoasters were made. Some were made of wood, like this one. But more were made of steel.

Steel rollercoasters

The first steel rollercoaster was made in the USA.

It was made in 1959 and you can still ride it today!

People liked the first steel rollercoaster. So more and more were made.

Matterhorn Mountain, Fantasyland, Disneyland USA

Canyon Blaster, Adventure Dome, Las Vegas USA

Today, there are hundreds of steel rollercoasters.

Some are like this one. They have lots of bends and loops.

The trains on rides like this go upside-down and loop-the-loop!

And some steel rollercoasters are like this one.

Rides like this have trains that hang down from the track.

On this Vampire Ride in the UK, the trains have no floor.

There are rollercoasters you stand up in.

There are some rollercoaster rides that spin as you ride.

And there are some rollercoasters that can make you fly! What will rollercoasters do next?

Six of the best in the UK

Here are six of the best UK rollercoasters. Check out how tall they are and see how fast they go.

This is The Big One at Blackpool Pleasure Beach.

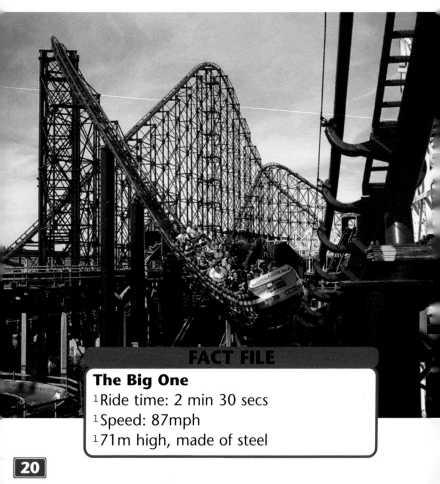

FACT FILE

The Big One
[1] Ride time: 2 min 30 secs
[1] Speed: 87mph
[1] 71m high, made of steel

This is Shockwave at Drayton
Manor Park, built in 1994. It is a
stand-up rollercoaster. It goes
upside-down 4 times!

FACT FILE

Shockwave
[1]Ride time: 1 min 20 secs
[1]Speed: 53mph
[1]36m high, made of steel

This big rollercoaster ride is Megafobia at Oakwood Park in Wales.

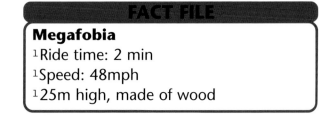

FACT FILE

Megafobia
[1]Ride time: 2 min
[1]Speed: 48mph
[1]25m high, made of wood

This rollercoaster at Chessington is Dragon's Fury. It has 9 cars. The cars spin as you ride!

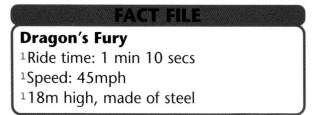

FACT FILE

Dragon's Fury
[1]Ride time: 1 min 10 secs
[1]Speed: 45mph
[1]18m high, made of steel

This is Nemesis at Alton Towers. It cost £10 million to make this ride.

FACT FILE

Nemesis
[1]Ride time: 2 min 55 secs
[1]Speed: 50mph
[1]13m high, made of steel

This is Colossus at Thorpe Park.

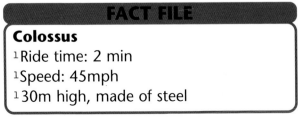

FACT FILE

Colossus
1 Ride time: 2 min
1 Speed: 45mph
1 30m high, made of steel

Here are some of the best rollercoasters in the USA.

Check out if they are made of wood or steel and see how long the rides last.

This is Millennium Force at Cedar Point, Ohio. This steel rollercoaster is one of the tallest in the world!

FACT FILE

Millennium Force
[1] Ride time: 1 min 45 secs
[1] Speed: 93mph
[1] 94m high, made of steel

This is Goliath at Six Flags Magic Mountain, Valencia. It was made in 2000.

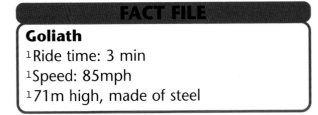

FACT FILE

Goliath
[1] Ride time: 3 min
[1] Speed: 85mph
[1] 71m high, made of steel

This is The Beast at King's Island, Ohio. It has 3 trains of 6 cars. It is the longest wooden rollercoaster in the world!

FACT FILE

The Beast
[1] Ride time: 3 min 40 secs
[1] Speed: 64mph
[1] 32m high, made of wood

This is The Son of Beast. There is just one wooden rollercoaster in the world with a loop – and this is it!

Son of Beast
[1] Ride time: 2 min 20 secs
[1] Speed: 78mph
[1] 66m high, made of wood

This is the Incredible Hulk at Islands of Adventure, Ohio. It has three trains.

FACT FILE

Incredible Hulk
[1]Ride time: 2 min 15 secs
[1]Speed: 67mph
[1]33m high, made of steel

This is Thunderbolt at Kennywood, West Mifflin. It is an old wooden rollercoaster but it is still one of the best!

FACT FILE

Thunderbolt
[1] Ride time: 1 min 30 secs
[1] Speed: 55mph
[1] 21m high, made of wood

Index

Cover: Kingda Ka © coasterclub.org.

Images pp.1, 4-5, 25 Colossus © EMPICS. Images pp.6-7 Kingda Ka p.16 Matterhorn Mountain, p.18, pp.21-24 © coasterclub.org. Images p.10 Montu, p.17 Canyon Blaster, pp.28-31 © coasterimage.com. Images p.12 Giant Dipper; p.15 The Racer, p.27, p.30 by Eric Gieszl © UltimateRollercoaster.com. Image p.20 reproduced courtesy of Blackpool Pleasure Beach. Image p.26 reproduced courtesy of Cedar Point amusement park/resort.

With thanks to Andy Hine MBE, RCCGB; Justin Garvanovic, ECC; Sarah Jane Wright, Blackpool Pleasure Beach and Bryan Edwards, Cedar Point.